FROGS & TOADS

by Jane Dallinger and Sylvia A. Johnson

Photographs by Hiroshi Tanemura

A Lerner Natural Science Book

Lerner Publications Company • Minneapolis

Sylvia A. Johnson, Series Editor

Translation by Joe and Hiroko McDermott

Photographs on pages 4, 8, 16 (left), 39 (left),
40 (bottom right), and 43 by Klaus Paysan

The publisher wishes to thank Kevin Marx,
Assistant in Zoology, The Science Museum of Minnesota,
for his assistance in the preparation of this book.

This book is available in two editions:
Library binding by Lerner Publications Company
Soft cover by First Avenue Editions
241 First Avenue North
Minneapolis, Minnesota 55401

LIBRARY OF CONGRESS CATALOGING-IN-PUBLICATION DATA

Dallinger, Jane.
   Frogs and toads.

   (A Lerner natural science book)
   Adapted from The birth of frogs and toads, by H.
Tanemura, originally published under title: Kaeru no
tanjō.
   Includes index.
   Summary: Text and photographs describe the trans-
formation of tadpoles into mature frogs and toads.
   1. Frogs — Juvenile literature. 2. Toads — Juvenile
literature. [1. Frogs. 2. Toads] I. Johnson, Sylvia A.,
joint author. II. Tanemura, Hiroshi. III. Tanemura,
Hiroshi. Kaeru no tanjō. English. IV. Title V. Series:
Lerner natural science book.
QL668.E2D27   597.8'7043   80-27667
ISBN 0-8225-1454-0 (lib. bdg.)
ISBN 0-8225-9502-8 (pbk.)

This edition first published 1982 by Lerner Publications Company.
Revised text copyright © 1982 by Lerner Publications Company.
Photographs copyright © 1972 by Hiroshi Tanemura.
Adapted from THE BIRTH OF FROGS AND TOADS copyright © 1972
by Hiroshi Tanemura. English translation rights arranged with Akane Shobo
Company, Ltd., through Japan Foreign-Rights Centre

All rights to this edition reserved by Lerner Publications Company.
International copyright secured. Manufactured in the United States of America.

International Standard Book Number: 0-8225-1454-0 (lib. bdg.)
International Standard Book Number: 0-8225-9502-8 (pbk.)
Library of Congress Catalog Card Number: 80-27667

6 7 8 9 10 11 12 13 14 15 99 98 97 96 95 94 93 92 91 90

A Note on Scientific Classification

The animals in this book are sometimes called by their scientific names as well as by their common English names. These scientific names are part of the system of **classification**, which is used by scientists all over the world. Classification is a method of showing how different animals (and plants) are related to each other. Animals that are alike are grouped together and given the same scientific name.

Those animals that are very much like one another belong to the same **species** (SPEE-sheez). This is the basic group in the system of classification. An animal's species name is made up of two words in Latin or Greek. For example, the species name of the lion is *Panthera leo*. This scientific name is the same in all parts of the world, even though an animal may have many different common names.

The next group in scientific classification is the **genus** (GEE-nus). A genus is made up of more than one species. Animals that belong to the same genus are closely related but are not as much alike as the members of the same species. The lion belongs to the genus *Panthera*, along with its close relatives the leopard, *Panthera pardus*, the tiger, *Panthera tigris*, and the jaguar, *Panthera onca*. As you can see, the first part of the species name identifies the animal's genus.

Just as a genus is made up of several species, a **family** is made up of more than one genus. Animals that belong to the same family are generally similar but have some important differences. Lions, leopards, tigers, and jaguars all belong to the family Felidae, a group that also includes cheetahs and domestic cats.

Families of animals are parts of even larger groups in the system of classification. This system is a useful tool both for scientists and for people who want to learn about the world of nature.

The common European frog (*Rana temporaria*)

Frogs and toads are close relatives, and they are alike in many ways. Most of them spend part of their life in water and part on land. Their bodies are generally similar in shape, and they eat similar kinds of foods. Frogs and toads are both **cold-blooded*** animals. This means that their body temperature changes as the temperature of their surroundings changes.

There are differences between frogs and toads too. Adult frogs spend more time in the water than adult toads. Frogs have smooth skin, are slender in build, and have long hind legs. These powerful hind legs make it possible for some frogs to jump great distances. Most toads have rough skin, round bodies, and short legs. They usually move with short hops. As adults, they spend more time on land than many frogs.

*Words in **bold type** are defined in the glossary at the end of the book.

Left: **A young frog rests on top of an adult.**

Frogs and toads belong to a class of animals known as **amphibians** (am-FIB-ee-unz). Most amphibians spend the first part of their lives in the water, swimming and breathing like fish. As adults, they can move about on land and breathe air, so they spend less time in water.

Frogs and toads begin their lives as eggs. After they hatch, they are called **tadpoles**. Tadpoles live in the water and breathe through gills. But as they grow, their bodies change in many ways. By the time they have become adult frogs and toads, they are able to live on land and breathe air through lungs. The great change that takes place during the development of amphibians is known as **metamorphosis** (met-uh-MOR-fuh-sis).

As you read this book, you will learn more about how amphibians grow and live. The descriptions given here are true of most frogs and toads, but not all of them. For example, most frogs begin life in the water, but some do not. So remember as you read that each type of frog or toad is a little different than any other type.

A toad in the shallow water of a pond

In northern countries, spring is the time of year when amphibians mate and lay eggs. During the day, toads and frogs hide under fallen leaves or in shallow holes to keep their skin moist. In the evening, they travel toward water in order to mate and lay their eggs. Late at night, hundreds of frogs and toads coming from many directions may gather in one pond. The males usually arrive at the pond before the females.

Some male frogs and toads have only one vocal sac (above left), while others have two (above right and opposite).

After reaching the water, a male frog or toad begins to make sounds to attract a female. These sounds are usually called **croaking**, and they are produced by an amphibian's vocal cords. Air passes over the vocal cords on its way from the amphibian's lungs to its mouth. When air rushes into the mouth, it causes the **vocal sacs** to puff up. Vocal sacs are pouches of skin that act as "echo chambers" for the sounds made by the vocal cords. As air goes rapidly back and forth between the lungs and the vocal sacs, the loud croaking sound occurs.

Two toads mating. The male is on top of the female.

On a spring night, a pond may be crowded with many different kinds of male frogs and toads, all croaking loudly to attract mates. When the females arrive at the pond, they have to find partners of their own species. They are able to do this because each species of frog and toad has its own special mating call.

When a female hears the call of a male of her species, she approaches him. The male climbs on top of the female and holds on to her with his front legs. The female lays her eggs in the water, and at the same time, the male releases sperm that fertilizes them. After a female has laid her eggs, she leaves the pond. A male frog or toad may stay and try to find another partner.

Some frogs and toads lay only a few eggs, but most species lay hundreds and even thousands of eggs at one time. Only a few of these eggs will live to become adults. Eggs and tadpoles are eaten by other amphibians and by fish, birds, and insects. Frogs and toads must lay many eggs to make sure that some will survive to become adults.

A toad in a pond surrounded by strings of eggs

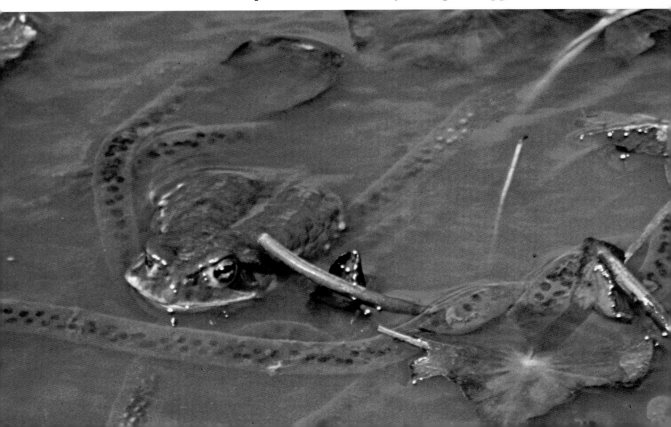

Left: Eggs just after laying, before the jelly absorbs water

Below: Strings of toad eggs inside their jelly covering

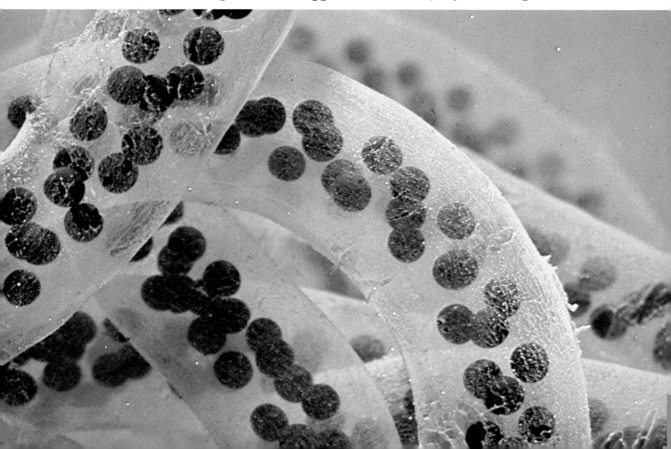

Frog and toad eggs are covered by a jelly-like substance. The jelly helps to keep the eggs moist, and it also protects them from injury. Toad eggs leave the female's body connected together in long strings of jelly. Frog eggs are laid separately. Some frog eggs stick to underwater plants, while others float together in large bunches.

Shortly after the eggs are laid, the protective jelly absorbs water and swells up. Each egg is neatly arranged inside the jelly with its darkest part on top. This dark area protects the egg from receiving too much sunlight, which might damage it.

An amphibian egg is usually about 1/12 inch (2 millimeters) in diameter when it is laid. This small speck contains everything needed to produce a new frog or toad.

The egg of an amphibian, like the eggs of other animals, consists of a single cell. This cell has two important parts. The largest part is the **yolk**, which will serve as food for the developing amphibian. The part of the cell that will become the amphibian itself is the **nucleus** (NYU-klee-uhs).

The development of a new frog or toad begins when the nucleus of a male amphibian's sperm cell unites with, or fertilizes, the nucleus of a female's egg cell. When this happens, the egg cell begins to divide. It becomes two cells, then four cells, then eight, and so on. This cluster of dividing cells is the **embryo** (EM-bree-oh), the first stage in the development of a new frog or toad.

The photographs on the next few pages show the development of toad eggs. The pictures were taken through a microscope so that you can see the cells dividing and the embryos beginning to grow.

The time it takes for amphibian eggs to develop is different for different species of frogs and toads. Some amphibian embryos are ready to hatch in one day, while others take several days or even weeks to develop completely. The toad embryos shown here will take seven days to reach the next stage of their development.

These toad eggs have just been laid. Each egg is a single cell surrounded by a jelly-like covering.

Three hours after laying, each single cell has divided into 2 cells. The fertilized eggs have now become embryos, the first stage in the development of new toads.

Four hours after laying, the 2 cells of the embryos have divided again. Each embryo is now made up of 4 cells. The grooves in the embryos mark the edges of the individual cells.

Six hours after laying, each embryo has 16 cells.

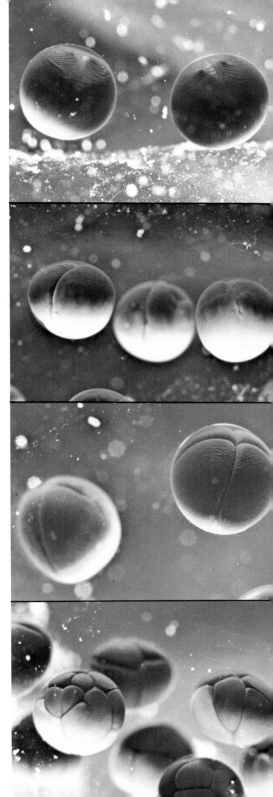

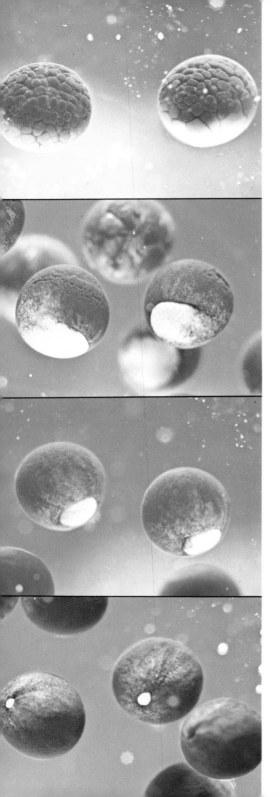

Ten hours after laying, each embryo has become a kind of ball made up of layers of cells. The top part of the ball is hollow. The bottom part contains the yolk.

Embryos on the second day after laying. The bright, round area at the bottom of each embryo is the part of the yolk that can be seen from outside the ball of cells. This is called the **yolk plug**.

As the embryos continue to grow, the yolk plugs become smaller. At the same time, more and more layers of cells develop. These layers will become different parts of the embryos' bodies.

During the third day, the yolk plugs gradually disappear. Now the yolks cannot be seen from outside the balls of cells. But they are still inside, providing food for the growing embryos.

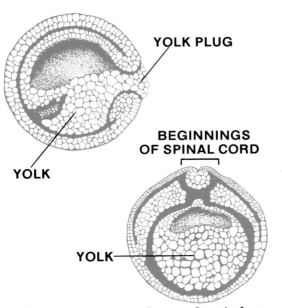

YOLK PLUG

YOLK

BEGINNINGS
OF SPINAL CORD

YOLK

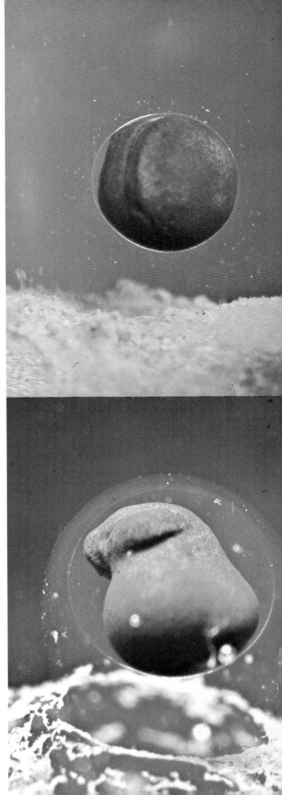

These drawings show what is happening inside the embryo. In the top drawing, the yolk plug has almost disappeared. The bottom drawing shows the development of the embryo's nervous system.

By the end of the third day, the embryo's nervous system has begun to form. The ridges that can be seen in the top picture are the beginnings of the spinal cord.

By the fourth day, the embryo's head is taking shape. Its eyes and mouth are forming. Inside the embryo's body, the digestive system and the blood system are developing.

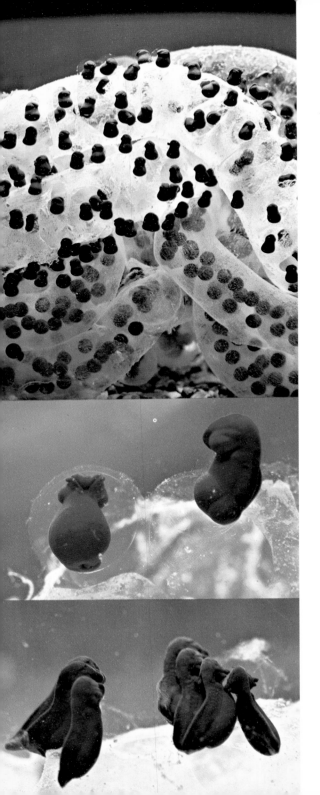

Now it is the seventh day after the toad eggs were laid. The embryos have hatched from their eggs and are floating up out of the strings of jelly (left). They have now become tadpoles. The tadpoles can't swim yet. They can only float together and stick to weeds in the water.

By the tenth day after the eggs were laid, the tadpoles have developed gills on both sides of their heads (right). Gills are organs used for breathing in water. They pick up oxygen from the water and bring it into a tadpole's body through the blood system.

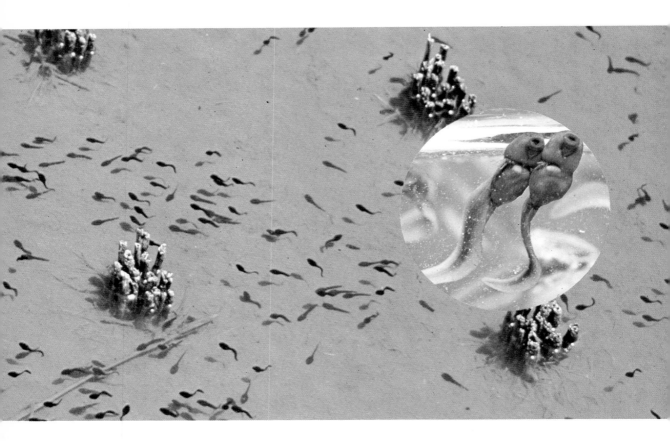

During the second week after egg laying, the tadpoles go through more changes. Skin grows over the gills to protect them. Their tails get longer and are now strong enough to be used for swimming (above).

While tadpoles are growing, they need a lot of food. Their main food is **algae** (AL-jee), simple plants that grow in water. Using their mouths, tadpoles scrape algae off rocks or weeds under the water. A tadpole's mouth makes a good scraping tool. It has sharp jaws and tiny teeth made out of a horn-like material.

For a while, the outward appearance of tadpoles stays the same. But six weeks after they hatch, tiny swellings appear on both sides of the body, near the base of the tail (left). These swellings develop into short hind legs with paddle-shaped feet. As the tadpoles' hind legs grow longer, the feet take shape and the divisions between the toes gradually appear (right).

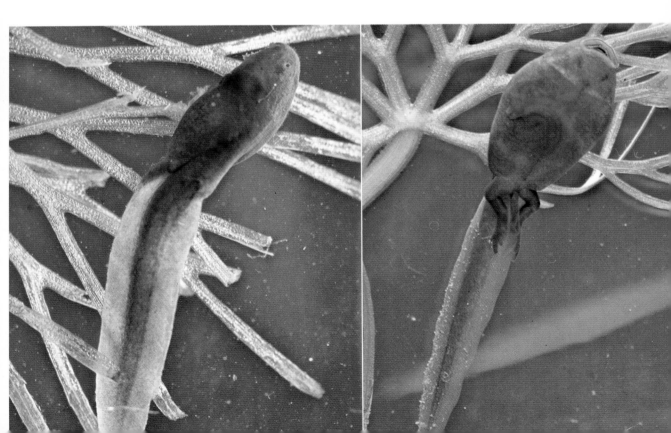

The front legs of tadpoles develop two weeks after the hind legs. Unlike the hind legs, the front legs begin their development inside the body. As they grow, they come out through the gill openings. Usually the right leg pushes through to the outside first. The left leg follows later. (In the picture above, the tadpole on the left has one leg out. The one on the right has both of its front legs out.)

During this time, many other changes are taking place inside the bodies of tadpoles. For example, the digestive system is getting shorter and changing in other ways. These

changes make it possible for the plant-eating tadpoles to become meat-eating toads.

After its legs have developed, a tadpole is almost ready to become a young toad. Its tail is shrinking and will soon disappear (left). The tadpole's face has begun to look more like the face of an adult toad. Its eyes are puffed up, and its wide mouth stretches around to the sides of its head. Its nostrils are developing. Inside, the gills have been replaced by lungs. The tadpole can now breathe through its nose. It is almost ready to begin living on land.

These tadpoles have been caught in a pond that has dried up. Most of them will die because they have not developed to the point where they can live on land.

The metamorphosis of these two young frogs will not be complete until their tails disappear completely.

When they are ready to live on land, young toads and frogs are usually less than 1 inch (2.5 centimeters) long. Some frogs and toads grow to their full size within one year. Others may take up to five years to reach their full size. Adult frogs and toads range from 1/12 inch to 10 inches (1.25 to 25 centimeters) in length.

Some frogs and toads live for many years. Frogs have been known to live for over 20 years. Records show that one toad lived for 36 years! But most amphibians die at younger ages.

Right: **A toad's thick skin does not lose moisture as easily as the skin of a frog.**

Even after they begin to live on land, many amphibians stay near water. Water is very important to amphibians because their skins have to be moist at all times.

Amphibians need moist skin for several different reasons. For one thing, frogs and toads take water into their bodies through their skins. They don't drink with their mouths as humans and many other animals do. Moist skin is also important because of the way that amphibians breathe. Adult frogs and toads use their lungs to take oxygen from the air, but they also get some oxygen from the moisture on their skins. Without this supply of oxygen, amphibians could not live.

It is not hard to see why an amphibian is in trouble if its skin dries out. The skin of most frogs dries out very easily, and this is why frogs usually stay near bodies of water. Toads have skin that does not lose moisture so easily. For this reason, toads can live farther away from water than most frogs.

If they are not near a pond or puddle, frogs and toads have other ways of keeping their skin wet. They can soak up the night dew. Or they can dig holes in the ground and lie in the damp soil.

Frogs that live near water are excellent swimmers. To swim, they pull their hind legs close to their bodies and then kick them back. Stretching out, they glide forward through the water. The pictures above show the way that frogs swim.

The "frog kick" is also used by humans. If you know how to swim using the frog kick, you can move your legs much like frogs move their legs in the water.

The webs that many frogs have between their toes help to make them good swimmers. As a frog's hind legs kick back, the toes spread apart. The webs stretch open and push against the water. Some human swimmers use rubber flippers that push against the water just like a frog's web.

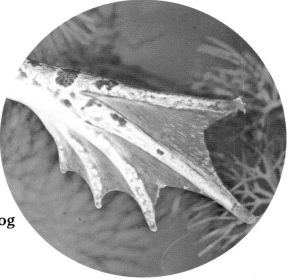

The webbed foot of a frog

A toad swallowing a moth

After they become adults, frogs and toads eat only meat. Their favorite foods are tiny creatures like snails, flies, water beetles, mosquitoes, worms, and dragonflies. Amphibians will only eat food that is alive and moving. If they are given a dead insect, they ignore it. When frogs and toads are kept as pets, their owners usually have to catch live insects to feed them.

Frogs and toads usually use their tongues to catch their food. An amphibian's tongue is attached at the front of its mouth, not at the back, as human tongues are. The tongue is long, and the end of it is very sticky.

The pictures on this page show how a toad uses its tongue to catch an insect. When the toad sees the insect, it flops its tongue out of its mouth. The insect gets stuck on the sticky end. Then the toad flops its tongue back in and gulps down its meal.

Snakes are some of the
most dangerous enemies
of frogs and toads.

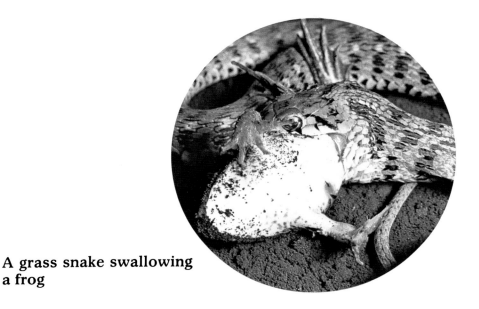

**A grass snake swallowing
a frog**

When frogs and toads eat insects, they are acting as **predators** (PRED-uh-ters) in the world of nature. Predators are animals that hunt and eat other animals. But sometimes frogs and toads get eaten themselves. Then they become the **prey** (PRAY) in the chain of natural life.

Snakes, large water beetles and water scorpions, catfish, and otters are some of the predators that eat frogs and toads. Many birds also prey on amphibians. Hawks, crows, and owls eat frogs and toads whenever they have a chance. Large wading birds like cranes and herons also catch amphibians in the shallow waters of ponds and lakes.

Frogs and toads are sometimes able to avoid the predators that hunt them. One way is by not being seen. The colors of many amphibians make it possible for them to blend in

with their surroundings. A frog's green skin may match the greenish water of a shallow pond or the green leaves of trees. Toads with brownish, bumpy skin are hard to see against a background of earth and twigs.

A few amphibians have skin colors and patterns that change. These changes are caused by such things as differences in temperature and in the amount of sunlight and moisture in their surroundings. The pictures on these two pages were taken of the same tree frog under four different sets of conditions. You can see how the color and pattern of the frog's skin have changed from picture to picture. This ability to change color helps an amphibian to blend in with its surroundings and to avoid being seen by predators.

During the winter months in northern countries, predators have a hard time finding frogs and toads. That is because the amphibians are hidden away in holes and underground burrows. They are spending the winter in the inactive state of **hibernation** (hi-bur-NAY-shun).

Because amphibians are cold-blooded animals, their body temperatures fall during cold winter weather. Amphibians are not warm enough to keep up their normal activities at this time of year. So they hibernate in burrows at the bottom of ponds, on hillsides, or in other places. Their breathing, heartbeat, and other body functions slow down. Because they are inactive, they need very little food. Amphibians can live for months on the food already stored in their bodies.

When spring's warmer days begin, frogs and toads come out of hibernation. They go to ponds to mate, and once more eggs begin to grow into new frogs and toads.

A toad hibernating in a burrow

There are more than 2,500 kinds of frogs and toads. They live in almost all parts of the world, except in the regions around the North Pole and South Pole. On the following pages, you can read about some of these amphibians.

Above left: The spring frog (*Rana dalmatina*) is a member of the family Ranidae. Frogs of this family are very common all over the world. The spring frog is famous for its jumping ability. It can make long leaps of several feet.

Above right: The common European toad (*Bufo bufo*) belongs to the family Bufonidae. Members of this family live on every continent except Australia. Like all toads, the common European toad has a thick body, short legs, and dry bumpy skin.

Top left: The common European frog (*Rana temporaria*) lives in northern and central Europe. It is even found in the cold regions north of the Arctic Circle.

Top right: The common American bullfrog (*Rana catesbiena*) lives in many parts of the United States. It is the largest American frog, normally reaching six or seven inches (20 centimeters) in length. Bullfrogs are so big that they can catch and eat young birds and fish.

Middle left: The African clawed frog (*Xenopis laevis*) is found in south and east Africa. These frogs spend most of their lives in the water. When searching for food, they use their clawed toes to stir up mud on the bottoms of ponds.

Middle right: The northern leopard frog (*Rana pipiens*) lives throughout southern Canada and the northern United States. The pattern of spots on the frog's skin gives this species its common name.

Bottom left: Poison-arrow frogs belong to the family Dendrobatidae. These frogs live in the jungles of Central and South America. Their skin holds a poisonous liquid that protects them against predators. Indians of the region also use the poison from the frogs' skin. They kill a frog and hold it over a fire so that the poison drips from its skin. Then they collect the poison and dip their hunting arrows in it.

Bottom right: The edible frog (*Rana esculenta*) is found throughout Europe. Frog legs are a popular food in some European countries, and edible frogs often end up on the dinner table. Frog meat tastes much like chicken.

Top: Fire-bellied toads (genus *Bombina*) are found in Europe and Asia. These toads are a dull grayish color on top. If a predator approaches, they raise their bodies to show their brightly colored undersides. These bright colors serve as a warning to predators. Fire-bellied toads have poison in their skins. Any animal that tries to eat one of these toads will find that it has a very unpleasant taste. After such an experience, the animal will stay away from fire-bellied toads when it sees their bright warning colors.

The fire-bellied toad in the picture on the top left lives in northeast Asia. Its scientific name is *Bombina orientalis*. On the right is the European fire-bellied toad (*Bombina bombina*).

Bottom left: Spadefoot toads live in North America, Europe, and tropical Asia. They belong to the family Pelobatidae. This family's common name comes from the hard, horn-like growths found on the hind feet of some spadefoots. These "spades" are used as digging tools. Spadefoots of Europe and North America spend most of their lives in hollows and holes that they dig in the ground. They travel to ponds and puddles of water only during the mating season.

Bottom right: The midwife toad (*Alytes obstetricans*) lives in Europe. This species has a very unusual way of taking care of its eggs. The toads mate on dry land. After the female lays her eggs, the male attaches the strings of eggs to his hind legs. He carries the eggs around for several weeks, sometimes dipping them in water to keep them moist. When the eggs are ready to hatch, the toad releases them in a pond.

These two tree frogs are natives of Japan. Like most frogs that live in trees, they have round, padded toes that help them to cling to branches. They move through the treetops, catching insects for food.

Both of these frogs belong to the family Rhacophoridae. Some members of this family do not spend any part of their lives in water. When the adults are ready to lay their eggs, they make nests out of foam on the ground. The foam gets hard on the outside, but inside, it is soft and filled with liquid. Within the foam nests, the frog eggs hatch into tadpoles, and the tadpoles become young frogs.

44

GLOSSARY

algae — simple plants that grow in water or in damp places

amphibians — cold-blooded animals that usually begin their lives in water, taking in oxygen through gills. As adults, most amphibians have lungs and live on land.

cold-blooded — having a body temperature that changes as the temperature of an animal's surroundings changes

croaking — the sound made by male frogs and toads during the mating season

embryo — an animal in an early stage of development, before birth or hatching

gills — organs used to take in oxygen under water. Tadpoles have gills, adult frogs and toads do not.

hibernation — an inactive state during which an animal's body functions slow down. In northern countries, frogs and toads spend the winter in this state.

metamorphosis — an extreme change in the appearance and habits of an animal. In frogs and toads, the change is from a tadpole that lives in water into an adult that lives on land.

nucleus—the most important part of a cell, containing the material that controls growth and cell division

predator—an animal that hunts and eats another animal

prey—an animal that is hunted and eaten by another animal

tadpole—an early stage in the development of frogs and toads. When a frog or toad embryo hatches from the egg, it becomes a tadpole.

vocal sac—a stretchy pouch of skin in the lower part of a male amphibian's mouth. When vocal sacs are filled with air from the lungs, they magnify the sounds made by an amphibian's vocal cords.

yolk—the part of an egg that provides food for the growing embryo

yolk plug—the part of the yolk that can be seen from outside the developing embryo. The yolk plug becomes smaller as the embryo grows.

INDEX